IF FOUND PLEASE RETURN TO:

Greater Than a Tourist Book Series
Reviews from Readers

I think the series is wonderful and beneficial for tourists to get information before visiting the city.

-Seckin Zumbul, Izmir Turkey

I am a world traveler who has read many trip guides but this one really made a difference for me. I would call it a heartfelt creation of a local guide expert instead of just a guide.

-Susy, Isla Holbox, Mexico

New to the area like me, this is a must have!

 -Joe, Bloomington, USA

This is a good series that gets down to it when looking for things to do at your destination without having to read a novel for just a few ideas.

-Rachel, Monterey, USA

Good information to have to plan my trip to this destination.

-Pennie Farrell, Mexico

Great ideas for a port day.

-Mary Martin USA

Aptly titled, you won't just be a tourist after reading this book. You'll be greater than a tourist!

-Alan Warner, Grand Rapids, USA

Even though I only have three days to spend in San Miguel in an upcoming visit, I will use the author's suggestions to guide some of my time there. An easy read - with chapters named to guide me in directions I want to go.

-Robert Catapano, USA

Great insights from a local perspective! Useful information and a very good value!

-Sarah, USA

This series provides an in-depth experience through the eyes of a local. Reading these series will help you to travel the city in with confidence and it'll make your journey a unique one.

-Andrew Teoh, Ipoh, Malaysia

GREATER THAN A TOURIST- AMERICAN SOUTHWEST USA

50 Travel Tips from a Local

Julia McDonnell

Cover designed by: Ivana Stamenkovic
Cover Image: https://pixabay.com/en/rocks-american-southwest-184267/

Edited by:

CZYK Publishing Since 2011.

Greater Than a Tourist
Visit our website at www.GreaterThanaTourist.com

Lock Haven, PA

ISBN: 9781724106827

>TOURIST

50 TRAVEL TIPS FROM A LOCAL

BOOK DESCRIPTION

Are you excited about planning your next trip?

Do you want to try something new?

Would you like some guidance from a local?

If you answered yes to any of these questions, then this Greater Than a Tourist book is for you.

Greater Than a Tourist- American Southwest by Julia McDonnell offers the inside scoop on the American South West. Most travel books tell you how to travel like a tourist. Although there is nothing wrong with that, as part of the Greater Than a Tourist series, this book will give you travel tips from someone who has lived at your next travel destination.

In these pages, you will discover advice that will help you throughout your stay. This book will not tell you exact addresses or store hours but instead will give you excitement and knowledge from a local that you may not find in other smaller print travel books.

Travel like a local. Slow down, stay in one place, and get to know the people and the culture. By the time you finish this book, you will be eager and prepared to travel to your next destination.

TABLE OF CONTENTS

DEDICATION

This book is dedicated to my husband, Tommy, who lovingly supports my wanderlust - encouraging and participating, sometimes following my lead, sometimes taking the lead and always holding my hand as we travel along our path filled with adventures.

ABOUT THE AUTHOR

Julia McDonnell grew up in the American Southwest. She has lived most of her life there while traveling extensively througout the country, across the borders into Canada and Mexico, and throughout Europe. Her wanderlust developed at an early age while traveling and vacationing with her family and continues to grow, fueled by her passion for exploring, discovering and experiencing fun places, great food and new adventures. She currently lives in Arizona, the heart of the American Southwest.

HOW TO USE THIS BOOK

The Greater Than a Tourist book series was written by someone who has lived in an area for over three months. The goal of this book is to help travelers either dream or experience different locations by providing opinions from a local. The author has made suggestions based on their own experiences. Please do your own research before traveling to the area in case the suggested places are unavailable.

FROM THE PUBLISHER

Traveling can be one of the most important parts of a person's life. The anticipation and memories that you have are some of the best. As a publisher of the Greater Than a Tourist book series, as well as the popular 50 Things to Know book series, we strive to help you learn about new places, spark your imagination, and inspire you. Wherever you are and whatever you do I wish you safe, fun, and inspiring travel.

Lisa Rusczyk Ed. D.
CZYK Publishing

OUR STORY

Traveling is a passion of the "Greater than a Tourist" series creator. Lisa studied abroad in college, and for their honeymoon Lisa and her husband toured Europe. During her travels to Malta, an older man tried to give her some advice based on his own experience living on the island since he was a young boy. She was not sure if she should talk to the stranger but was interested in his advice. When traveling to some places she was wary to talk to locals because she was afraid that they weren't being genuine. Through her travels, Lisa learned how much locals had to share with tourists. Lisa created the "Greater Than a Tourist" book series to help connect people with locals. A topic that locals are very passionate about sharing.

WELCOME TO
> TOURIST

INTRODUCTION

"I believe the world is incomprehensibly beautiful - an endless prospect of magic and wonder."

— Ansel Adams

Welcome to the American Southwest! This magnificent region of diverse scenery and landscapes encompasses the lower south and west area of the United States. Anchored by the states of Arizona and New Mexico, the American Southwest includes areas of the states of Colorado, Utah, Nevada, California and Texas to the border with Mexico.

Most people think of the American Southwest as desert - a vast expanse of barren desolate land - hot and dry. It may come as a surprise that the American Southwest also incorporates snowy mountain peaks, rivers, lakes, and lush forests.

The American Southwest is beautiful, breathtaking and mesmerizing. It is also a harsh and challenging environment.

1. LAND OF EXTREMES

The American Southwest is a land of extremes with elevations from 282 feet below sea level in Death Valley, California, to over 12,000 feet in Flagstaff, Arizona.

The southwest is a Semi-Arid climate with at least 5 different climate zones. It has hot dry weather with very little rainfall to cold freezing temperatures and snow. The average rainfall varies from 3 inches a year to 40 inches a year. In some areas of the desert, the temperature can range from extreme daytime heat over 100°F to an extreme nighttime cold of 32°F all on the same day!

From the vast desert floor to the high mountain peaks, there are expanses of prickly cactus and thorny mesquite to forests of fragrant pines and junipers. There are deep canyons and steep ravines, majestic rock monuments, high flat mesas, long winding rivers, and alluring seductive lake.

2. BE PREPARED!

When visiting the American Southwest be prepared for the extremes. Consider where you will be going, how long you plan on being there and what conditions you could/might possibly encounter.

These are Basic Essentials for your visit anywhere in the southwest:

WATER

Have at least One Liter of water - preferably two - per person. Include water for Pets (and a bowl). Have plenty of water for everyone. Always replenish water whenever you can.

SUN PROTECTION

Cover your head. Give your head a layer of insulation from the sun as in a hat. Baseball caps are popular and very easy to stash in the car. They have a bill (if worn properly) to shade the face. It has become fashionable to wear baseball caps backward. At least that shades the neck and if that is your preference… so be it. BEST: Broad-brimmed hats, even for the guys. A popular hat for a lot of people in the southwest is the domed-shape "lifeguard" straw hat with a wide brim.

Both the lifeguard style hats and baseball caps, along with other styles of hats can be purchased at gift shops, trading posts, convenience stores, and truck stops.

BANDANAS

Bandanas are good for a number of uses and are easy to have with you. You can also use a scarf or handkerchief. Tie them over your head for shade, around the forehead or neck to help with perspiration, or over your nose for dusty conditions. Bandanas can be soaked with water for added cooling to any of the previously mentioned uses. Bandanas are especially good to have with you if you get caught in a dusty situation - dust storms, trail rides, dirt roads, just like the cowboys - they knew!

Bandanas are also available at most trading posts, gift shops, convenience stores, and truck stops. Something to buy in a trading post - then you also have a souvenir!

SHOES, SOCKS, and SHIRTS

It's probably common sense and anyone who does much hiking will most likely be prepared with sturdy hiking shoes.

However, visitors who are not planning on hiking, but are jumping out of their vehicles to visit attractions, walk along paths at sites or take in the views at look-outs might be wearing just flip flops or sandals (that would be me!) and not realize how exposed they are to unexpected elements and possible hazards.

A better choice of footwear is some sort of closed-toed shoes (athletic shoes, hiking shoes or even closed-toed sandals) with socks to protect your feet from the hazards such as rocks, prickly cactus, small crawling critters, and insects at foot & ankle level, even HOT pavement. Asphalt and pavement can become so hot that flipflops are not much protection.

Wearing a long-sleeved shirt seems a bit contradictory in the sun and hot weather. It is a similar concept to wearing a hat. Covering your arms with a loose-fitting long-sleeved shirt will actually help you stay cool as well as protect your skin from the sun. The fabric absorbs perspiration and cools you off as it dries. Preferably white or light and a cotton material, but any long-sleeved shirt works. The key is "LOOSE-FITTING".

JACKETS

Heavier than a shirt, a jacket provides another layer of protection. Having a jacket available is always a good idea since the temperature might take a significant drop after the sun sets, or a thunderstorm or rain squall might develop with a downpour, cooling the air and getting you wet.

We learned the hard way when driving to Lake Havasu, AZ, one year for some spring break fun in the sun and water. We were excited about the predicted 100° days and packed swimsuits and shorts but no jackets or sweatshirts. We stopped at a look-out for a quick view over the Grand Canyon. It was a really quick view! At 6800 feet of elevation, it was still wintry. The wind was blowing, the sky was dark with clouds and the temperature was about 40°- it was cold! We ran to the edge, had a really quick look and scurried back to the car, deciding to visit the Grand Canyon another time when better prepared (which we have done). Have more than a shirt, have a sweatshirt, or better - HAVE A JACKET!

CELL PHONES

The world has become dependent on Cell Phones. However, in the wide open spaces of the southwest, cell phone service is spotty and in many places - NONEXISTANT- even along the major Interstate Highways. There are emergency phones along the Interstate Highways, but there are long stretches of many miles with NO cell service. Do not rely on your cell phone.

3. MELTING....
MELTING...MELTING....

NEVER EVER EVER leave anything in a vehicle that might melt or get too hot - especially living creatures - kids, dogs, cats, birds, grandpa -and especially in the summer, even in the higher mountain elevations and EVEN with a window cracked. Full open window - maybe.

The interior of a vehicle heats up higher than you would ever think possible. With a comfortable 70°F outside temperature, inside the car, the temperature becomes 89°F in just ten minutes. During the summer months with outside temperatures of 100°F + the interior of your vehicle can get to 140°F+. Be Cautious! Water can get hot enough to make tea and be almost too hot to drink. Be very careful with anything plastic such as DVDs and cassette tapes, CD cases etc. And Cell PHONES! Mine has gotten so hot, it shut down with a warning of being overheated. That happened when I left my phone in the car and it wasn't even in the sun. Other susceptible items — Lotions, chapstick (will liquify). Of course groceries - your ice cream will melt!!

4. PETS

The American Southwest region - especially the lower elevations and desert - is harsh and can be life-threatening for pets. Most of the survival tips for people also apply to animals, except perhaps sunscreen…and hats, sunglasses, and shirts, although these I have actually seen on animals!

In general pets (dogs) are welcome. However, many sites restrict animals or at least have restricted areas for them. And there are Laws regarding pets.
OBEY THE RULES.

Leash Laws are in effect at public sites and attractions.

Be responsible for your pets and ALWAYS clean up after them.

Do not leave Pets in cars - It's the Law!
PET SAFETY

WATER! Have plenty of water for your pets and offer it to them often. Have a bowl and water just for pets. Whenever I drive with my dogs in the car, I always have a bowl filled with water. A sealable lid makes it easy to pop the lid and offer a drink without wasting water - water is precious in the southwest! I also have a convenient collapsible bowl (mine actually folds up and can be tucked in a back pocket) for walks and hiking. These are available at most pet stores.

Panting is the dog's way of cooling off and doesn't necessarily indicate thirst or being overheated - or it might! If you provide enough water often enough, you should know if the panting is just the

21

dog's cooling off mechanism or not. Always offer water. If they are thirsty, they will drink. My experience has been that dogs will also let you know when they are getting too hot by just lying down where they are or pulling you toward shade. Please pay attention to them and don't force them to move until they are refreshed.

Protect their Paws! Dogs are especially obedient and will do just about anything you ask them to and follow you anywhere - so please do not ask them to walk on the hot asphalt or pavement unless absolutely necessary. The asphalt is HOT! So are sidewalks. When you take your pet out for a walk, be very aware of the heat of the ground and consider their paws. If you think it's not too hot - take off your own shoes and socks and test it yourself with bare feet.

The wide open spaces and even the high country (forests) might seem ideal places to let your dog out for a run off the leash. Remember this is a harsh land and dogs may encounter unexpected danger as snakes, prickly cactus, and sharp rocks.

Never leave an animal in a vehicle. This is critical. The interior of a vehicle can rise to unbelievably extreme high temperatures - even with windows open, even in the high country, and even in the winter- remember you are still in the southwest. The sun is intense and quickly heats up the interior of a car!

There are Federal, State, and local laws that forbid leaving animals in vehicles. Anyone has the right to break a window to rescue an animal that appears to have been 'left' in a vehicle in adverse conditions.

We travel extensively with our dogs and they do very well. Be Aware. Take Precautions. You and your pets will all get along in the southwest.

5. SURVIVAL KIT

It is good to be prepared and keep the basic 'essential' items described above in your vehicle. It's also good to have a little bag or pouch - a container of some kind - to hold smaller items. These are non-essential items but strongly recommended. They might seem obvious but it is good to be reminded:

Sunglasses
Not critical but the sun is bright and it is a good idea to shade your eyes and give extra protection.

Sunscreen
Always a good idea, regardless of how much sun you think your skin can take.

Lip Balm
It's dry - keep lips moist to prevent dry chapped lips or excess licking which causes chapping.

Salty Snacks
Any simple snacks but especially salty snacks - chips, sunflower seeds, popcorn. BEST:

23

Snacks with more protein or nutrition such as mixed nuts, trail mix, granola bars, energy bars. This may not be the time to limit salt, so consider 'lightly' salted if necessary.

Cell Phone Chargers

Have an extra cell phone charger. Consider a solar-powered charger. There is lots of sun and not many electrical outlets! As Cell Phones (and other technological equipment -tablets, laptops, etc) search for service, their power drains quickly and they need charging more often.

First Aid Kit

A First Aid Kit is recommended to have in any vehicle at any time but especially while traveling in the wide open country.

6. SURVIVING THE EXTREMES

WATER - WATER - WATER

Drink it, swim in it, cool off with it. Water is not just for hydration however, hydration is the #1 requirement! And water is not just for the desert.

"It's HOT but it's a DRY heat". Dry is the key word here. Hot or Cold, the southwest climate is still DRY and you need to stay hydrated. Low desert or high Mountains - Drink LOTS of water.

Stay hydrated with water - other liquids and beverages are acceptable if there is nothing else, however water is the best!

If you are thirsty - you are already dehydrated. If you are NOT thirsty, you may be severely dehydrated!

Sweating? Perspiring? - take your pick … they are the same thing! Your body is trying to regulate its temperature and cool itself by sweating/perspiring. With the evaporation of the sweat/perspiration, you feel cooler. A breeze helps the process but also dries you out faster - your body is still dehydrating. Not sweating/perspiring? Sometimes, you don't realize you are sweating because it dries so quickly. You are dehydrated - DRINK WATER until you begin to sweat! You need to replenish the fluids - water!

Some places have water that is 'non-potable' - that means 'not for drinking'. It is safe to use for cooling off engines, radiators, - even bodies but not considered safe to drink.

COOLING OFF

If you find yourself overheated - Water First! Find water and get in it. If you cannot get to a large enough body of water such as a river or lake or even a swimming pool, you can bring your temperature back down by taking a shower or even just sitting with your feet in water - a bucket, tub or even a child's inflatable swimming pool.

If you begin feeling over-heated while out on a hike, especially in the summer in the desert and there is no substantial amount of water, do the wet T-shirt thing and dampen or soak your shirt with water and wear it wet - the evaporation as it dries helps cool

you off. If you have two shirts --or can go bare-chested (men only except in extreme conditions and necessity. Women need to be cautious of laws regarding indecent exposure!) --wrap your head with a wet shirt (or towel or scarf).
SHADE

Seek shade - even the shadow of a cactus will provide some relief from the hot sun - just don't sit too close or use it for a backrest!

Provide your own shade: a hat - umbrella - paper bags … something to provide a shadow and protection from the sun.

No hat? No Problem! Wrap something around your head. If you have a bandana, scarf, an extra shirt, or go bare-chested (again - with caution women). You've heard the expression of wearing a paper bag over your head? Well, now is a good time —not to hide from shame but from the sun and to give yourself a bit of 'shade'. Poke a couple eye-holes to be able to see. I have actually seen people using paper of all types to shade their heads —bags, newspapers, cardboard, and such.

7. HEAT EXHAUSTION

Be alert to signs and symptoms of being overheated and dehydrated. Both can sneak up on you. Heat exhaustion - Heat Stroke - Sun Stroke are all synonymous for severe heat illness caused when the body temperature gets too high due to high temperatures. It can also result from physical exertion. Be extra cautious with physical exertion IN hot weather!

You might not feel thirsty and won't realize you are becoming dehydrated -- a good reason to sip water frequently.

Be alert to other signs or symptoms such as red, dry or damp skin, nausea, headache, dizziness, lethargy, confusion, and lack of thirst. If you begin feeling weak, shaky, light-headed physically 'off'… get cooled off as soon as you can!

8. BELIEVE THE SIGNS!

NO SERVICES.

Even on the Interstate Highways, there are some areas of long distances (40 -100 miles) between services. That means there will not be any gas stations, convenience stores, toilets, restaurants, etc.

STAY ON THE PATH
NO CLIMBING
DO NOT PICK UP ARTIFACTS
NO PHOTOS OF RELIGIOUS CEREMONIES

These signs and others are for your own safety as much as they are for the respect of the land (National Monuments, Parks, and Forests), and of the native people and their traditions.

FLASH FLOOD AREA, SEEK HIGHER GROUND.

Thunderstorms cause local flooding and runoffs and rushing water. Seek higher ground

27

and stay out of low areas - especially if you are caught in a heavy downpour. Flash floods are serious and can happen without a cloud in the sky. It might be raining at higher elevations. I have witnessed vehicles floating down washes and across roads. I have also seen vehicles submerged in underpasses. Do not cross water on the roads! It might not appear deep or fast moving - don't risk it!

9. SEASONS IN THE SUN

Weather conditions in the American Southwest are as varied and diverse as the landscape and elevations. They can change quickly, especially in the summer.
MONSOONS
        The 'monsoon' season in the southwest generally refers to the summer months when the humidity is higher. It is not a period of ongoing drenching rain as associated with the Asian countries. When the humidity rises, the heat feels hotter. With the higher humidity, clouds will form and rain will fall but rarely reach the ground in the lower elevations. We do experience occasional rain storms which can be drenching. They are usually very short downpours but can have lots of water and cause flooding. Rain 'squalls' in the desert are usually isolated. The higher elevations - the mountains - will get rainfall and thunderstorms almost every day.
HABOOBS
        Desert dust storms - often referred to as Haboobs - are a phenomenon that is amazing to see

and experience but not really much fun. They are often referred to as 'rolling' dust storms. From afar and from above they appear as a huge wall or wave of dust rolling across the open desert picking up speed - and more dust - gaining momentum. Once they "arrive" or "land" they subside - meeting the resistance of buildings and trees, similar to a hurricane making landfall. Once the wind settles, so does the dust - sifting down and setting on everything. It's quiet - like the 'eye' of the storm. I have seen vehicles in carports with inches of dust settled on them, appearing to have been abandoned and forgotten under years of dust. The settling dust can also appear as fog making visibility low, especially at night. It is best to find shelter indoors. When driving, it is best to pull over to the side of the road as visibility can be zero. This same caution applies to rain storms. Sometimes these Haboobs or dust storms can be seen arriving, other times, they come in with no initial/apparent warning. Sometimes they are announced with winds that pick up and get stronger and carry debris.

GULLY WASHERS and FLASH FLOODS

These are real and they are serious! Often the rain is a torrential downpour in a short amount of time. The average annual rainfall for most of the southwest is only a few inches, but those few inches can arrive all at once in one storm bringing a fast build-up of water that doesn't soak in quickly causing flooding of streets as well as flooding of any canyon, gully, 'wash', and arroyo, which is how most of those were formed.

Get to high ground and stay out of low areas like underpasses or even just dips in a road. The water can be fierce. The force of the flowing water and the depth of it can be deceiving. I have witnessed vehicles 'floating' down streets and in the gullies and washes. Also, remember that the storms are more frequent in the higher elevations. Even if you are not actually experiencing rainfall, the water from storms in the mountains will seek the lowest level and will cause flash flooding at the lower elevations.

10. PLANES. TRAINS, AND AUTOMOBILES

Since the American Southwest is a vast area of land covering a huge portion of the United States, you can approach it from many different directions and in different modes of transportation.

By Plane

Fly into one of the major airports in the southwest, and rent a car. Soon you will be on your adventure of exploring the American Southwest. Major cities (Las Vegas, NV, Phoenix, AZ, Albuquerque, NM) and towns (Palm Springs, CA, Tucson and Yuma, AZ, Roswell, NM) have International airports. Most towns have regional or municipal airports or at least runways.   By Train

Sit back and watch the breathtaking beauty of spectacular landscapes unfolding as you cross

sections of the great American Southwest, traveling in comfort on board a train. You will have opportunities to disembark at stops along the way and explore the towns or stay longer and visit nearby attractions. Or make connections with other train routes for more adventure and see other parts of the southwest.
By Automobile

BEST! Get the most out of your visit to the southwest by automobile. Whether you arrive by airplane or train and rent a car, or arrive in your own vehicle, the best way to experience the American Southwest is to drive.
By Bus - Public Transportation

Public transportation is minimal. In the larger cities, there are city transit systems. Travel between some cities is offered by intercity coach services such as Greyhound, and specialized motorcoach tour companies. Train service is limited to long-distance schedules.

11. SURVIVAL GUIDE – DRIVING

Be Prepared!

There are some very important tips and additional cautions you should know BEFORE heading out in your vehicle. Even if you are planning on just viewing the scenery from the comfort of your vehicle while traveling along the Interstates and not getting too far off the main road, these tips are important.
GAS

Keep the gas tank full. It costs the same to drive off the top half as the bottom half and in the southwest, it is a lot safer! Those long stretches of highway between services are sometimes more frequent on the Interstate Highways than the back road where you might find a small gas station in a little dusty town.

FUEL UP IN ARIZONA
Traveling between Arizona and California, buy gas on the Arizona side if you can. Gas is notoriously more expensive in California. On the Interstate Highways, there are towns and truck stops on both sides of the state line. On secondary roads, the choices are fewer, but you can still calculate "topping off the tank" on the Arizona side.
WATER!
Always have water in the car! Always have EXTRA water in the car, even on the Interstates. If for any reason you get stopped or stranded (road construction or obstructions) for any length of time - it is good to have extra water with you. A gallon jug in the trunk is easy to carry and good insurance.

Best: Purchase a 1-gallon jug of water at a grocery store for about $1.00 and refill water bottles. This is more economical - and easier on the environment than buying one bottle at a time or packing a case of smaller bottles.
WATCH THOSE SIGNS!
Watch the signs, pay attention and have faith! Sometimes you need to have a good sense of

direction, other times you need to have faith in the signs.

INTERSTATE 10 travels East-West except in Arizona, between Tucson and Phoenix where it actually goes North-South. Driving from Phoenix to Tucson on I-10, you will be going west (into the setting sun). Follow the signs for I-10 East Tucson which will take you south! Have faith!

HIGHWAY 95 is another tricky/quirky situation. This is between Califonia and Arizona. US Highway 95 travels through California between Blythe on I-10 and Needles on I-40. AZ Highway 95 travels through Arizona between Quartzsite on I-10 and I-40 east of Needles at the 9-Mile Marker and sign for traveling south to Lake Havasu City and Parker. These two highways are about 25 miles apart. Pay attention!

12. PLACES TO GO, THINGS TO DO AND SEE

As diverse as its scenery, climate, and elevations are, the American Southwest offers an abundance of equally diverse adventures, activities, and intrigue.

Outdoor Recreation
Exploring
History
Geography & Geology
Plants
Wildlife
Birding

What is your interest? You will find it here in the American Southwest!

13. HIGHWAYS AND BYWAYS

If you want to take the fast road, there are multiple Interstate Highways that traverse the American Southwest.

If you have the time and are planning an extended visit and slower paced exploration, a myriad of byways and back roads will take you further away from civilization and deeper into the deserts, hills, and mountains of the southwest.

When we travel, we like to be flexible, allowing extra time to follow a back road or visit an unexpected discovery. We usually travel without much of an itinerary or schedule. My favorite way of traveling is to seek places that are off the beaten paths, away from the main roads. Not all of the fun places we find are on back roads but are often on by-ways and out-of-the-way places.

14. THE MOTHER ROAD – GET YOUR KICKS

Despite its reputation - and because of it - Route 66 - the Mother Road (also known as U.S. Route 66, US 66, the Main Street of American and the Will Rogers Highway) is a fun route to follow through the southwest.

Much of the original road disappeared when the Interstate System took over but there are still portions of the road designated as National Scenic Byways or "Historic Route 66". You can still 'get your kicks' along sections of it.

One of my favorite byways of Route 66 is between Ashfork and Kingman in Arizona. Here, sections of the old road are still visible, and drivable, as it parallels I-40. Stop in Seligman at the Snow-Cap Drive-in for a hamburger or soft-serve ice cream cone while enjoying a display of nostalgic paraphernalia. On down the road, the town Peach Springs is the administrative headquarters of the Hualapai (wha-lah-pie) people. Near Peach Spring, is the entrance to the Grand Canyon Caverns, as well as the trailhead of Hualapai Hilltop for a hike into the canyon.

Other little towns along the route, Nelson, Truxton, Valenine, and Hackberry offer minimal services. Hackberry has a display of vintage cars and more paraphernalia. Watch for the "Burma Shave" signs. They are refreshed periodically with different sayings just as they were when Route 66 was the main road "back in the day".

15. 'X' MARKS THE SPOT

This is definitely worth a stop especially if you have children who would love being able to 'stand' in 4 states at once. No children? Even without children - let the child within come out and play on the corner of 4 states. The monument, a granite disk embedded into the ground, legally marks the spot where the states of Colorado, Utah, Arizona, and New Mexico join. It is the only point in the United States where this occurs. It is also the boundary point between the Navajo Nation and the Ute Mountain Ute Tribe (no - not a typo: they are a tribe of the Ute nation)

The Four Corners Monument is maintained by the Navajo Nation as a tourist attraction. Depending on the time of the year, Native American vendors offer their arts and handicrafts, and sometimes food items. It is best to plan on services (gas, motel, restaurant) at towns along the way.

16. BELIEVE IT OR NOT

The crash of a UFO at Roswell NM in 1947 has been a topic of debate and controversy with purported military cover-ups and classified programs. True or not, the alleged incident is intriguing and attracts UFO, Sci-Fi, and Alien enthusiasts. Join the believers as well as the skeptics who gather at the annual UFO Festival and Galacticon in July to revel and celebrate anything and everything Sci-Fi. Costumes and craziness are fun and I am intrigued with UFOs and other space-related activities, however, I prefer visiting Roswell other times of the year avoiding the festival-goers.

As a site of secret experiments, record-breaking rocket launches, and a successful balloon flight into and back from the stratosphere, Roswell has had on-going space connections beyond UFO crashes. Learn more of Roswell's connection with outer space at the Roswell Museum and Art Center's "Cradle of Space Exploration" exhibit.

17. SHIPS IN THE DESERT

Shiprock

Imagine seeing a clipper ship off in the distance, sailing across the landscape — of the desert! Shiprock is an impressive rock formation towering 1583 feet above the desert and is visible for miles and miles around.

This fascinating rock is what is left of a volcano 'throat' that has been shaped by erosion over time. I am thrilled every time I see it. Easily visible for miles, keep watching it as you get closer and then pass on by as it changes appearance from different sides.

The Navajo Nation considers their "Rock with Wings" (Shiprock) a religious site. Getting up close is possible but a little tricky and only necessary if it is really important to you. It is on private property - the sacred lands of the Navajo Nation - and it is a religious site. All climbing is banned. This massive rock is impressive from the nearest highways (US

491& US 64). If you are determined to get up close, respect that it is a sacred site to the Navajo people. There are no services, no museum, or trading post. The town of Shiprock is about 15 miles from the rock formation.

Earthships

Still looking for UFO's? You might think you've found a landing site when you see the Earthships near Taos, NM. This community of odd and unusually shaped structures gives an appearance of having arrived from another planet. Earthships are the ultimate recycled home - or more specifically UPcycled. Mostly built out of dirt and old tires and lots of cans and bottles, the structures take on futuristic and other-worldly shapes and designs. I find them exciting and fascinating. The concept of living off-grid in a passive solar home with conveniences of conventional homes plus luxuries like indoor vegetable and fruit gardens is intriguing. Since my initial visit, the community has grown. There is now a visitor center and rentals are available providing opportunities to experience life inside an Earthship.

18. COLORFUL ALBUQUERQUE

Albuquerque, New Mexico, is a colorful start for your visit to the American Southwest if you are coming from the east or north-central area. A major city in the southwest region, Albuquerque is a mix of old and new, offering all things of a modern city while being rich with Indian and western heritage.

I especially enjoy Old Town Albuquerque with the historic adobe buildings surrounding Old Town Plaza. Stroll the boardwalk, shop in the galleries and gift shops, visit museums. Take your pick of one of the many restaurants and savor the unique flavors of New Mexican cuisine or just pick a bench in the plaza and relax in the shade.

19. SANDIA TRAM

For a spectacular view over the landscape of New Mexico, experience an exhilarating ride on the Sandia Peak Tram on the east side of Albuquerque. It is the longest aerial tram in the United States, ascending 3,819 ft up the steep western side of the Sandia Mountains.

20. BURSTS OF COLOR

Experience a different view over the New Mexico landscape from the basket of a hot air balloon. The mild temperatures, calm winds, and clear blue skies provide near-perfect conditions for frequent and long hot air balloon flights. Daily flights are offered year-round by numerous local companies. If you prefer to stay grounded, you can enjoy watchingnthe hot air balloons from any vantage point in the area.

39

BEST: October is when the sky of Albuquerque bursts with color as it fills with hot air balloons during the magical Albuquerque International Balloon Fiesta. If you've seen other balloon festivals, and think you've seen enough, think again! You haven't seen anything until you see the Albuquerque sky bursting with colored balloons. The Albuquerque Balloon Festival is considered to be the world's largest hot air balloon festival, with hundreds of balloons of all colors, shapes, and sizes from all over the world filling the sky at any one time. Camping is available. And camping close to some of the launch areas is amazing! Close enough to walk among the balloons and watch them fill and lift off. We woke up to the sound of the balloons filling and lifting off and stepped outside the camper to see the thrilling sight of a sky full of balloons right overhead. Pure magic!

21. KALEIDOSCOPE OF COLOR

The historical Gathering of Nations Powwow is another profusion of color. Fill your heart and soul with the kaleidoscope of colors, the music, drumming, dancing, and spirit of this annual meeting of tribes. This Native American tradition of people gathering to celebrate life and friendships through dancing, singing, sharing stories continues through the Gathering of Nations Powwow. It is an exciting and spectacular experience of sights and sounds, arts and crafts and FOOD! It happens every year in Albuquerque on the fourth weekend in April. Make your plans and arrange for accommodations way ahead of time. There are LOTS of people in town that weekend! Be one of them!

22. SOPHISTICATED SANTA FE

North of Albuquerque off I-25, Santa Fe is the capital of New Mexico and the oldest state capital in the United States. It is also an upscale artist's colony with the traditional town plaza surrounded by galleries, gift shops, and museums. Santa Fe is a fun place to spend some time. I enjoy the sophisticated relaxed atmosphere. And I especially appreciate the town's specific construction guidelines maintaining the original style of low profile adobe structures. Even the State Capitol complies with a unique round design resembling th Zia Sun Symbol.The skylight in the rotunda is designed to resemble an Indian basket weave. Worth a look!

We visited Sante Fe seeking original works of art by the well-known American artist, Georgia O'Keefe, who lived and painted in this area. We were thrilled to be in her domain, to see the landscape from which she drew inspiration and get to view her artwork. Tours of her home, Abiquiu (aba-kew) are available by appointment. The museum is just a few blocks from the town plaza.

23. TAOS – TOWN AND PUEBLO

North of Santa Fe is the town of Taos, New Mexico where the traditional town plaza is the center of activity. The drive north from Santa Fe to Taos is one of the prettiest we've driven, taking you along the river and into the trees. At nearly 7,000 feet elevation, Taos has lots of winter activities available at multiple ski resorts within close proximity of the town.

While visiting friends who live near Taos, we participated in a 'street show' of classic cars lining the streets around the plaza. We enjoyed entertainment by local musicians and delicious food offered by the local eateries. We wandered through shops and galleries.

At the edge of the town of Taos is the Taos Pueblo, a UNESCO World Heritage Site. This is a place I was curious about and excited to visit. Taos Pueblo is one of the oldest continuously inhabited communities in the United States and is considered to be one of the most private, secretive and conservative of the pueblos.

On my first visit, I had a sense that I was intruding. The people are friendly and welcome visitors but are reserved, appearing shy. It is important to understand that visiting the pueblo is the same as visiting their private homes. Be respectful. And be careful - only enter buildings and doors that indicate public entrance. You do not want to make the mistake of walking into a private home.

There are very strict guidelines about photography. Always ask permission to photograph -

especially a tribal member - and never take a photo without their permission.

Sometimes the Pueblo closes for cultural or religious observations so, as with all public attractions, check before going to the pueblo to confirm that it is open to the public.

24. ACOMA PUEBLO

Another opportunity to learn the history of southwest Indians and experience an inhabited pueblo is to visit the Acoma Pueblo. It is located about 60 miles west of Albuquerque on I-40 on top of a 367-foot bluff. Acoma Pueblo IS considered the oldest continually inhabited community in North America. Both the Mission and the Pueblo are Registered National Historic Landmarks and are on the National Register of Historic Places.

Also a visitor-friendly pueblo, the Acoma People are less reserved and more open about their lives, providing opportunities to learn about their customs, traditions, art, and culture with educational tours and exhibits.

Again, respect their customs, traditions, and homes. And as always, check before going for any possible unexpected closures.

25. ANCIENT INHABITANTS

The American Southwest is abundant with archaeological evidence of people who lived in the area in 'ancient' times. These Indian 'ruins' and petroglyphs offer fascinating insights into their existence. One of the most well-known sites is the Cliff Dwellings of Mesa Verde National Park in southern Colorado. Scattered over the entire southwest region, cliff dwellings, excavations, and petroglyphs can be found. Follow the "Trail of the Ancients" through northwestern New Mexico, where evidence abounds. Or discover other sites on your own. They are all worth visiting.

26. HOMOLOVI INDIAN RUINS

The abundance of Indian ruins in the southwestern region is a bit like castles and cathedrals in Europe. They each are unique with their own beauty and history but after a while, they become a bit 'ho-hum' as they begin to blend together. Not so with Homolovi (homo-lo-vee) State Park! This is one of the ancient sites we happened on and deserves a spot on your itinerary.

One summer, we took to the higher elevations to enjoy the cooler weather and enjoy some camping and sightseeing. We found ourselves on our own trail of ancient Indian dwellings. Homolovi is not difficult to find or on a backroad by-way. It is easily accessed from I-40 north of Winslow, AZ. It is a state park with camping facilities, a gift shop, and a museum. Homolovi is impressive with over 300 ancestral Puebloan excavated sites so far. It is a 'live dig'. Archaeological excavation is on-going. It is fun to be at a site that is still being excavated and new discoveries are being made.

27. LOOK BUT DON'T TOUCH!

In many national and state parks, forests, and ancient ruins, you will see signs warning you to not pick up or take anything - any artifacts- including small seemingly insignificant pottery chards. We had never seen anything even an insignificant pottery chard until we visited Homolovi State Park. There are pottery chards everywhere you look and step - as if the pottery was shattered and scattered like confetti! Still, don't touch — just look…and be amazed!

28. DAMMED RIVERS

The Colorado and Rio Grande Rivers are the major rivers in the American Southwest. Both start in the Rocky Mountains of Colorado and flow into Mexico, one into the Sea of Cortez on the west and the other into the Gulf of Mexico on the east.

Development along both rivers through Colorado and Mexico created more and more demand for water to supply towns that were springing up and farmlands that needed irrigating. The Colorado and Rio Grande Rivers were dammed and they have been dammed so many times along the way that they are merely wetlands where they meet the ocean.

29. DAM RESULTS

Many lakes and reservoirs were created by the dams along the rivers and are popular recreational areas for all things water related and more.

COLORADO RIVER

On the Colorado River are three major lakes and top destinations for extensive water-play. Lake Powell, created by the Glen Canyon Dam in northern Arizona stretches north between Utah and Arizona. Lake Mead, created by Hoover Dam (previously known as Boulder Dam) is near Las Vegas, NV. And Lake Havasu, created by the Parker Dam, forms the border between California and Arizona. Bring your own or rent personal watercraft and houseboats, or go on a guided boat tour for 'on the water' experiences. Once I learned to water ski, I could hardly get enough of it. These lakes offer seemingly endless stretches where you can ski for miles - if you have the stamina! - and beautiful coves with gloriously flat water.

RIO GRANDE RIVER

Reservoirs and recreation areas along the Rio Grande River are on a smaller scale than those on the Colorado River. Some reservoirs are water storage only. Most waterways offer great kayaking and canoeing, and white water rafting opportunities.

In addition to water recreation, there are many wildlife refuges and great birding opportunities. And remember — you are in the Southwest. Along the rivers and lakes are more evidences of the ancients. Often, Cliff dwellings, petroglyphs, and Indian ruins can be seen from the water or within easy hiking distance from the water's edge.

30. SALTY SEAS AND CELEBRITIES

When traveling between Arizona and California on Interstate 10, give yourself a little extra time to take in some sights along the stretch of highway near the resort city of Palm Springs. If driving from either Arizona or further west in California, you will be ready to get out and stretch your legs.

The Salton Sea is an unusual body of shallow salty water in the middle of the arid desert, a curious creation formed by a breach in a dike on the Colorado River, miles away in the early 1900s. It is below sea level but 5 ft higher than the lowest point in Death Valley.

The Salton Sea is a little underwhelming and yet fascinating at the same time. If you really want it on your list of sites seen then definitely plan an hour or two for the visit. Be prepared for brackish water, dead fish, bubbling mud pots and an odor, described by the US Geological Survey as "objectionable", "noxious", "unique", and "pervasive".

Getting there from I-10 at Indio, follow the signs to Mecca. Feeling adventurous? Going either to or from the Salton Sea, take the byway between Chiriaco Summit east of Indio and Mecca for a drive through Box Canyon and some gorgeous scenery and rock formations.

The resort city of Palm Springs offers year-round golfing and other fair-weather recreation. It became popular in the 1930s with movie stars and celebrities flocked to this desert oasis for the dry weather, hot springs, spas, and recreation. It continues to be a popular destination for winter visitors, retirees, and weekend wanderers.

For a bit of a nostalgia, drive through Palm Springs, exit I-10 at either end on US 111- the 'old' highway'. Watch for Kirk Douglas Way, Dinah Shore Dr, Gene Autry Trail, Frank Sinatra Dr, Gerald Ford Dr, and Bob Hope Drive. Or stay on I-10 and memorialize Sonny Bono (who also served as mayor of Palm Springs and as a US senator) with a drive along the Sonny Bono Memorial Freeway section past Palm Springs.

31. SELFIE WITH THE DINOS

From the west end of the Sonny Bono Memorial Freeway section of I-10, "Dinny" and "Mr. Rex" are easily visible and easily accessible. Exit at Cabazon and grab a Selfie with these giant dinosaur sculptures (150-foot-long /150-ton Dinny and 65-foot-tall/ 100-ton Mr. Rex). These iconic roadside attractions were originally built to lure customers into a roadside restaurant and gained even more fame for their appearance in Tim Burtons' film: Pee-wee's Big Adventure.

32. MILKSHAKES AND MOVIES

My preferred stop along this stretch of I-10 by Palm Springs is the Shield's Date Garden. Slurp a Date Shake while being entertained with a short documentary - "THE SEX LIFE OF A DATE" - and stock up on dates to take home or snack on along the rest of your trip. Located on the 'old' highway US-111 at Indios.

33. FORMIDABLE AND FASCINATING

Hot is hot - Death Valley or not. However, Death Valley has a reputation of being one of the hottest places in the world. Driving between Las Vegas and Los Angeles on Interstate 15 you can get a sense of Death Valley. Take the byway and actually experience it.

Hot or cold, at 282 feet (86m) below sea level, it is the lowest place in the American Southwest. Death Valley National Park encompasses most of this desert valley and offers incredible scenery and variety of terrain and activities. There are sand dunes, volcanic flows, 'natural bridge' rock formations, and expansive vistas. There are short hikes and long hikes, scenic drives, and views without hiking, day trips and campsites for longer trips. Fortunately, with its designation as a National Park, there are visitor centers, outposts, improved services, and paved roads. It is still Death Valley. The fear associated with Death Valley before we had faster vehicles (with air-conditioning) and more services and conveniences available, is still valid!

Caution is always advised when adventuring into the Death Valley area. ALWAYS-ALWAYS-ALWAYS, have water with you and extra water in your vehicle. Even if walking a short distance from your vehicle - always take plenty of water! Dehydration happens quickly and you can become disoriented with the extra exertion of hiking or even just walking. You may not always be in sight of your vehicle or campsite so keep focused on landmarks. Remember there is NO CELL service in these wide-open desert spaces.

In these types of extreme conditions, it is always a good idea to let someone know where you plan on going and how long you plan to be there. If hiking away from your vehicle in a parking lot or from a campsite, leave a note of where you plan to go, when you leave and when you plan to return.

34. ST. GEORGE AND THE VIRGIN RIVER

St George could be considered Three-Corners as it is nearly but not directly on the boundary point of three states (Utah, Arizona, and Nevada). It is also near the transition zone of three geographical areas - The Mojave Desert, the Colorado Plateau, and the Great Basin. It doesn't need that designation to attract visitors. The climate in St George aligns with the hot summers temperatures (over 100°F) and milder winters of the desert making it a popular destination for winter visitors. I have been in St. George when there was snow covering everything.

Another one of my favorite drives is on Interstate 15 in the southwest corner of Utah. A fun winding drive through the Virgin River Gorge is a relatively short drive with a rapid change in elevation. In and out of shade in the narrow canyon and crossing over the river several times, it is beautiful any time of the year and any time of the day. It is a little tricky if there has been any snow - and yes there can be snow in this area!

35. ST. GEORGE AND THE DINOSAURS

St. George, UT, has other attractions in addition to mild winters, stunning Red Cliffs… and pies. Inhabited by Anasazi, then Paiute Indians prior to European explorers, the area was first home to dinosaurs. Evidence of all the inhabitants is abundant with Indian ruins and petroglyphs, and dinosaur tracks. Check out the St George Dinosaur Discovery Site at Johnson Farm (right in the town) where thousands of dinosaur footprints are fossilized in a 200 million-year-old lake.

36. ST. GEORGE AND PIES!

I go to St George for another reason. I tend to 'travel by food' creating itineraries based on favorite foods I discover during my journeys. We discovered PIES in St George. Delicious "homemade" pies at Croshaw's Gourmet Pies on Bluff Street. Fresh-made daily right there in the store with real fruit fillings and no preservatives. The cream pies are heavenly. They also serve savory pies (meat pot pies) and quiches, and light lunch fare as in soups, salads, and sandwiches. We time our travels to be in St. George during Croshaw's business hours and always have a cooler in the car to take a pie with us! These are the BEST Pies - second only to my mother-in-law's! (She concurred during one of her trips with us!).

37. PRICKLEY PLANTS AND PRETTY FOWERS

The desert has a reputation for being hot, dry, and barren - devoid of life. In reality, it is a picturesque panorama filled with life. The life that survives the harsh conditions of the southwest is often prickly, spiky, tough, thorny and determined.

As tough and thorny as the desert appears, it has a softer delicate side. The desert is especially beautiful in the spring when cactus and trees are in bloom, and after a particularly rainy winter season when it comes alive with wildflowers. Cactus blossoms are usually only open for a few days, some just one day. They are quite fragrant and mostly at night.

The stately Saguaro (sah-war-oh) cactus is the multi-armed symbol of the American Southwest, often depicted as silhouetted in the sunset. In reality, the Saguaro cactus has very limited territory, growing only in the Sonoran Desert. It is slow growing, sometimes taking 75-100 years before developing an 'arm' and can be only 1.5 inches at 10 years old! Appearing most of the year as a tall serious sentry, in the spring, covered with large white blossoms, it appears lighthearted and playful.

In contrast, the Prickly Pear cactus, with short paddle-shaped pads instead of arms, is much less particular where it grows and can, be found everywhere in the west at all elevations, even next to a pine tree in the mountains. It produces abundant yellow flowers. Other cactus varieties offer flowers in a rainbow of colors.

The native Palo Verde trees burst with tiny yellow blossoms that drop to the desert floor creating a spectacular blanket of bright yellow in late spring and early summer depending on their elevation. The name Palo Verde translates from Spanish as "green pole/stick". These delightful trees appear frilly and almost delicate. They are survivors! They love the dry climate and survive without water by retaining needed chlorophyll for photosynthesis in the bark. They offer shade even without leaves with their multitude of small branches.

Palm trees are a common sight in the southwest. However, like many Snow Birds taking up residence and enjoying the southwest climate, some tropical plants such as palm trees have been introduced and easily adapted to the region as well. They are a friendly welcome sight in the stark desert landscapes, hinting at tropical breezes as they sway in the winds of southwest.

38. WILEY COYOTE AND FRIENDS

The American Southwest is also home to an array of animals. The coyote is perhaps the animal most people associate with the desert. The Coyote's amazing ability to adapt to its environment and habitat has perhaps earned it the reputation of being wilie (y-lee) or cunning. They live in all habitats from the scrub of the desert to foothills and even in and around large cities. They look like scraggy domestic dogs, are curious and are not very shy, appearing friendly...cunning? You might be tempted to coax them closer. Keep your distance and encourage them to do the same! And PLEASE - do not feed the animals! Let them stay wild. And keep your pets close by and on leashes, especially if you are camping but be cautious everywhere. And especially at night. However, I have seen coyotes walking down the street in my neighborhood in the middle of the day. I also have friends whose pets have been taken from their fenced yards - daytime and nighttime. Coyotes are known to easily jump 6-foot walls carrying off large dogs. Remember, the Coyote is strong and tough and adaptable. Coyotes are often depicted as "howling" at the moon. They often 'sing' at night with or without a moon. Their howls and barks and songs are a way of communicating with each other. It also provides a warning for you to be alert. They might be nearby.

39. HAVA-WHAT? JAVELINA!

An animal specific to the southwest is the Javelina (hava-leen-a). This animal looks similar to a pig but they are not even related. Often referred to as "musk hogs" because of their unpleasant odor, they are not wild hogs either. They are relatively common at the lower elevations, however we encountered Javelina in an Arizona campground at 7500 ft elevation, so be cautious anywhere in the southwest! Javelina are not particularly aggressive but can be, especially in protection of their young. You will also want to keep your dogs on leashes to be safe from Javelina as well as coyotes. They are not happy about dogs whom they consider a threat as a predator.

40. SNAKES, SCORPIONS, AND WALKING STICKS

Snakes and Scorpions, as well as Tarantulas, lizards, Gila monsters and even tortoises, are some of the other critters found in the southwest. Most of these you have to really look for but be cautious when camping and hiking. Always carry a walking stick - not so much for walking as for possible protection. Tapping a walking stick on the ground or poking under shrubs helps to alert these critters and gives you both a chance to change direction. Most animals, including these smaller ground crawlers, are not intentionally aggressive and would prefer to slither or crawl away than to attack. They rarely bite, strike or sting unless provoked or threatened.

SNAKES

The wide-open spaces and unique environment of the desert, as well as hiking trails in the mountains, and inviting green golf courses are all places you might encounter snakes. They like to lie in the sun warming themselves, especially in the spring and early summer when the sun is just starting to warm the earth or on warm days in the fall and winter. In the heat of summer, snakes become lethargic and listless appearing dormant and inactive. You might encounter one in the cool of a summer evening after the sun sets, and the temperatures are a little more bearable. Even if a snake appears sluggish or listless, it can spring to life quickly, especially if it is startled or harassed. Snakes do sleep at night.

The most common snake is the Diamondback Rattlesnake. However, the Mohave Rattlesnake is the most venomous. Rattlesnake bites are seldom fatal if treated promptly.

Rattlesnakes use the 'rattle' at the end of their bodies to warn others of their presence if they are cornered, or feel threatened. The rattle is a warning that they are about to strike. They do not need to be coiled to strike. They can strike from any position. If you hear a rattle, remember it is first a warning but don't take chances. If you don't actually see the snake, stop and remain very still, giving the snake an opportunity to move away or slowly retreat, especially if the snake is in view and you know you will be moving away from it.

SCORPIONS

A black light flashlight is a good item to add to your camping gear for the southwest, especially if you are planning to camp on the ground (in a tent) out under the stars.

Scorpions normally blend into their habitat and burrow into the dirt. They are very sensitive to sunlight and seek dark areas such as shoes, sleeping bags, and tents. Scorpions also glow in the dark under the UV rays of a black light. As an added caution, a black light flashlight can help make sure the coast is clear. They are also great for entertainment. Go for a night-hike and search for scorpions! Scorpions are not aggressive unless they feel threatened. Step over them or gently push them aside with a stick. If found in your gear where you'd rather they not be, toss them into the wild and they will find somewhere else to hide. Remember that you are intruding in their environment.

41. SNOWBIRDS

The milder climates and warmer winter weather of the southwest attract many visitors seeking refuge and respite from the long colder winters in the northern climates. Thousands of birds, as well as people, flock to the southwest to enjoy the mild temperatures and escape the cold and snow in the north.

The people are often referred to as Snow Birds The appropriate and polite reference is 'Winter Visitor'.

True 'snow birds' - the winged variety - travel thousands of miles to spend the winter in the southwest climate.

Huge flocks of Canadian geese can be seen following rivers as they wing their way north in the spring and south in the fall. Bald Eagles are more prevalent than the Golden Eagles in the desert southwest. Both are snowbirds, visiting the southwest in the winter to nest and have their young and can be seen perching on bare branches of trees.

42. HUMMERS IN HUACHUCA

Southeast Arizona is considered the Hummingbird capital of the United States. My favorite - the playful and friendly Hummingbirds provide endless

59

entertainment year round in most areas of the southwest. When some of their friends and relatives arrive for the winter, we enjoy their antics as they vie for dominance over the feeders, chasing and diving and whizzing past our heads.

Surprisingly, some of the best times to see abundant varieties of Hummingbirds are in July and particularly August. Ramsey Canyon in the Huachuca (hooah chooka) Mountains and Madera Canyon in the Santa Rita Mountains near Sierra Vista and Tucson are popular locations. As many as 15 species of hummingbirds can be seen frequently and dozens of other species pass through on their way to their breeding grounds in Mexico.

43. SEE THE CRANES

Other locations in this area, south, and east of Tucson are winter destinations for the annual migration of hundreds of other species of birds. Near the town of Wilcox, the impressive Sandhill Cranes gather by the thousands - reports are upwards of 30,000 birds at the peak of the migrations. These big birds, some with wingspans of 6 feet, have a history dating back over 2 million years. For me, it is a magnificent and almost haunting experience. With their loud trumpeting sound, they lift as a group at sunrise, filling the sky, off to feed in nearby fields.

They return in the late morning or early afternoon to settle in until the next day.

44. WINGS OVER WILLCOX

Wing your way over to Wilcox in January for The Wings Over Wilcox Birding and Nature Festival held annually in January. See the Sandhill Cranes and hundreds of other species of migrating birds wintering in the southeast of Arizona. Paid guided tours are available for more "up close and personal" opportunities. The tours sell out so book in advance.

45. BIG HOLE IN THE GROUND

Meteor Crater is a definite must! A worthy stop on your travels across I-40 in Arizona. We drove past this attraction numerous times, always curious but never taking time to visit. Finally, we decided to take a look and still can't believe we procrastinated. Talk about a big hole in the ground! It's not as big as the Grand Canyon which is often described by the unimpressed viewers as a big hole in the ground.

The Grand Canyon has taken millions of years to form through erosion by the Colorado River, wind, and weather. Meteor Crater took only a few seconds

50,000 years ago when an asteroid crashed into the earth.

To give visitors a perspective of the size of the Meteor Crater, a life-sized statue of an astronaut stands in the center at the bottom of the crater - try to find it without binoculars!

As if seeing this spectacular big hole in the ground isn't impressive enough - you get to actually touch a piece of the meteorite! And there is more — Take the Rim Tour - a fascinating way to experience the crater - view the crater from different look-out points, watch the movie and experience the simulated collision with sound effects. Learn more while being entertained with the interactive displays and exhibits. Visit the gift shop and rock shop. We camped at the RV Park located near the I-40 exit. It is convenient to the crater and offers the services of a gas station and country store. Remember — Water and Gas are essential in the southwestern region!

46. IF YOU HAVE TO ASK

Chilis (or chili peppers, hot peppers) are the foundation for most of the foods of the Southwest. Originating in Mexico, chilis found their way around the world and became a major flavor in many cultures There are numerous varieties of chilis in different sizes, colors, flavors and 'heat'. If you have to ask how hot or spicey a dish is - Proceed With Caution! What is hot to some is mild to others!

Flavors of the southwest are unique to the southwest. The cuisine varies only slightly by area. Limited to foods that could be gathered in the sparse, dry terrain or grown in the heat with minimal water, the unique flavors and foods of the Southwest have evolved over time with the rich heritage of the region.

Strongly influenced by the Spanish settlers blending European, Mexican and Native American foods and flavors the distinct dishes of the southwest developed.

47. FRY BREAD AND NAVAJO TACOS

Indian Fry Bread and Navajo Tacos are specialties of the southwest and a little safer on the spicy side. Fry Bread and Navajo Tacos are offered at roadside stands, visitor sites, and most festivals and street fairs throughout the southwest Fry Bread is just that - fried bread - pieces of leavened dough, fried or deep-fried and served plain or sweetened with a sprinkle of powdered sugar or drizzle of honey.

A deluxe offering of Fry Bread is a Navajo Taco (or Indian Taco). Fry Bread is topped with everything found in a taco - meat, cheese, lettuce, sour cream, salsa and pico de gallo ....delicious! Another word of caution: these are usually huge servings! My first Navajo Taco was at the Hualapai (wall-a-pie) Lodge in Peach Springs along Route 66 in Arizona. It was more than adequate for a filling lunch for two hungry people!

63

48. BANGLES, BOBBLES, AND BEADS

Everywhere you go, everywhere you look, you will see Indian jewelry, arts, and handicrafts offered for sale. Some of it is native-made and some isn't. Gallup, NM has the reputation of being the trading capital of the world for Indian-made jewelry and crafts.

Many of the Trading Posts in Gallup actually deal directly with the Native American people and offer truly authentic Indian-made jewelry, rugs, blankets, and other handicrafts both retail and wholesale. For the real deal - shop Gallup!

49. DESERT OR DESSERT?

Is it a desert or a dessert? The difference between desert and dessert? - we enjoy having two servings of dessert (double 'ss' in the spelling). Some of us enjoy an extra serving of the desert, too!

50. LOOK THROUGH DIFFERENT EYES

The first time visiting the southwest United States is an extraordinary experience. Driving across this wide open space and being able to see, sometimes for hundreds of miles, gives a sense of being able to see forever but there is always something on the horizon. Sometimes it seems like there is nothing out there but a barren desolate desert. Look again through different eyes. See the Dessert of the Desert. There is a unique beauty to this wide open space where you can literally see for hundreds of miles.

Look at the landscape and the terrain and imagine the Indians trekking across this vast territory or living high in the shelter of the rocks and the cliffs. Imagine the covered wagons jostling along and the cowboys on horseback making their way through the pricky cholla and cactus under the blazing hot sun or sitting by a campfire under a night sky of sparkling stars. Look at the different shades of green in the creosote bushes, sagebrush, and cacti; the colors of the sand, rocks, hills, and mountains; the shadows from wayward clouds. Watch for a summer rainstorm as it sweeps across the land in the distance. Keep an eye out for coyotes and road runners chasing around under the brush. Or watch the quail marching along in orderly fashion up and over rocks or an eagle or a vulture soaring over the landscape scouting for supper.

Beauty is in the eye of the beholder. To some of us who live and embrace these wild vast expanses, they are not barren and ugly, they are beautiful and full of life!.

TOP REASONS TO BOOK THIS TRIP

Landscape: Diverse scenery and topagraphy filled with an array of flora and fauna.

Climate: Generally temperate from mild winters to hot summers, great for outdoor activities year-round

History: Rich heritage of ancient inhabitants and western expansion.

Food: Flavorful foods unique to the American Southwest.

Recreation: Year-round opportunities for anyone's interest.

BONUS BOOK

50 THINGS TO KNOW ABOUT PACKING LIGHT FOR TRAVEL

PACK THE RIGHT WAY EVERY TIME

AUTHOR: MANIDIPA BHATTACHARYYA

Edited by Melanie Howthorne

ABOUT THE AUTHOR

Manidipa Bhattacharyya is a creative writer and editor, with an education in English literature and Linguistics. After working in the IT industry for seven long years she decided to call it quits and follow her heart instead. Manidipa has been ghost writing, editing, proof reading and doing secondary research services for many story tellers and article writers for about three years. She stays in Kolkata, India with her husband and a busy two year old. In her own time Manidipa enjoys travelling, photography and writing flash fiction.

Manidipa believes in travelling light and never carries anything that she couldn't haul herself on a trip. However, travelling with her child changed the scenario. She seemed to carry the entire world with her for the baby on the first two trips. But good sense prevailed and she is again working her way to becoming a light traveler, this time with a kid.

INTRODUCTION

He who would travel happily
must travel light.

-Antoine de Saint-Exupéry

Travel takes you to different places from seas and mountains to deserts and much more. In your travels you get to interact with different people and their cultures. You will, however, enjoy the sights and interact positively with these new people even more, if you are travelling light.

When you travel light your mind can be free from worry about your belongings. You do not have to spend precious vacation time waiting for your luggage to arrive after a long flight. There is be no chance of your bags going missing and the best part is that you need not pay a fee for checked baggage.

People who have mastered this art of packing light will root for you to take only one carry-on, wherever you go. However, many people can find it really hard to pack light. More so if you are travelling with children. Differentiating between "must have" and "just in case" items is the starting point. There will be ample shopping avenues at your destination which are just waiting to be explored.

This book will show you 'packing' in a new 'light' – pun intended – and help you to embrace light packing practices for all of your future travels.

Off to packing!

DEDICATION

I dedicate this book to all the travel buffs that I know, who have given me great insights into the contents of their backpacks.

THE RIGHT TRAVEL GEAR

1. CHOOSE YOUR TRAVEL GEAR CAREFULLY

While selecting your travel gear, pick items that are light weight, durable and most importantly, easy to carry. There are cases with wheels so you can drag them along – these are usually on the heavy side because of the trolley. Alternatively a backpack that you can carry comfortably on your back, or even a duffel bag that you can carry easily by hand or sling across your body are also great options. Whatever you choose, one thing to keep in mind is that the luggage itself should not weigh a ton, this will give you the flexibility to bring along one extra pair of shoes if you so desire.

2. CARRY THE MINIMUM NUMBER OF BAGS

Selecting light weight luggage is not everything. You need to restrict the number of bags you carry as well. One carry-on size bag is ideal for light travel. Most carriers allow one cabin baggage plus one purse, handbag or camera bag as long as it slides under the seat in front. So technically, you can carry two items of luggage without checking them in.

3. PACK ONE EXTRA BAG

Always pack one extra empty bag along with your essential items. This could be a very light weight duffel bag or even a sturdy tote bag which takes up minimal space. In the event that you end up buying a lot of souvenirs, you already have a handy bag to stuff all that into and do not have to spend time hunting for an appropriate bag.

I'm very strict with my packing and have everything in its right place. I never change a rule. I hardly use anything in the hotel room. I wheel my own wardrobe in and that's it.

Charlie Watts

CLOTHES & ACCESSORIES

4. PLAN AHEAD

Figure out in advance what you plan to do on your trip. That will help you to pick that one dress you need for the occasion. If you are going to attend a wedding then you have to carry formal wear. If not, you can ditch the gown for something lighter that will be comfortable during long walks or on the beach.

5. WEAR THAT JACKET

Remember that wearing items will not add extra luggage for your air travel. So wear that bulky jacket that you plan to carry for your trip. This saves space and can also help keep you warm during the chilly flight.

6. MIX AND MATCH

Carry clothes that can be interchangeably used to reinvent your look. Find one top that goes well with a couple of pairs of pants or skirts. Use tops, shirts and jackets wisely along with other accessories like a scarf or a stole to create a new look.

7. CHOOSE YOUR FABRIC WISELY

Stuffing clothes in cramped bags definitely takes its toll which results in wrinkles. It is best to carry wrinkle free, synthetic clothes or merino tops. This will eliminate the need for that small iron you usually bring along.

8. DITCH CLOTHES PACK UNDERWEAR

Pack more underwear and socks. These are the things that will give you a fresh feel even if you do not get a chance to wear fresh clothes. Moreover these are easy to wash and can be dried inside the hotel room itself.

9. CHOOSE DARK OVER LIGHT

While picking your clothes choose dark coloured ones. They are easy to colour coordinate and can last longer before needing a wash. Accidental food spills and dirt from the road are less visible on darker clothes.

10. WEAR YOUR JEANS

Take only one pair of Jeans with you, which you should wear on the flight. Remember to pick a pair that can be worn for sightseeing trips and is equally eloquent for dinner. You can add variety by adding light weight cargoes and chinos.

11. CARRY SMART ACCESSORIES

The right accessory can give you a fresh look even with the same old dress. An intelligent neck-piece, a couple of bright scarves, stoles or a sarong can be used in a number of ways to add variety to your clothing. These light weight beauties can double up as a nursing cover, a light blanket, beach wear, a modesty cover for visiting places of worship, and also makes for an enthralling game of peek-a-boo.

12. LEARN TO FOLD YOUR GARMENTS

Seasoned travellers all swear by rolling their clothes for compact and wrinkle free packing. Bundle packing, where you roll the clothes around a central object as if tying it up, is also a popular method of compact and wrinkle free packing. Stacking folded clothes one on top of another is a big no-no as it makes creases extreme and they are difficult to get rid of without ironing.

13. WASH YOUR DIRTY LAUNDRY

One of the ways to avoid carrying loads of clothes is to wash the clothes you carry. At some places you might get to use the laundry services or a Laundromat but if you are in a pinch, best solution is to wash them yourself. If that is the plan then carrying quick drying clothes is highly recommended, which most often also happen to be the wrinkle free variety.

14. LEAVE THOSE TOWELS BEHIND

Regular towels take up a lot of space, are heavy and take ages to dry out. If you are staying at hotels they will provide you with towels anyway. If you are travelling to a remote place, where the availability of towels look doubtful, carry a light weight travel towel of viscose material to do the job.

15. USE A COMPRESSION BAG

Compression bags are getting lots of recommendation now days from regular travellers. These are useful for saving space in your luggage when you have to pack bulky dresses. While packing for the return trip, get help from the hotel staff to arrange a vacuum cleaner.

FOOTWEAR

16. PUT ON YOUR HIKING BOOTS

If you have plans to go hiking or trekking during your trip, you will need those bulky hiking boots. The best way to carry them is to wear them on flight to save space and luggage weight. You can remove the boots once inside and be comfortable in your socks.

17. PICKING THE RIGHT SHOES

Shoes are often the bulkiest items, along with being the dainty if you are a female. They need care and take up a lot of space in your luggage. It is advisable therefore to pick shoes very carefully. If you plan to do a lot of walking and site seeing, then wearing a pair of comfortable walking shoes are a must. For more formal occasions you can carry durable, light weight flats which will not take up much space.

18. STUFF SHOES

If you happen to pack a pair of shoes, ensure you utilize their hollow insides. Tuck small items like rolled up socks or belts to save space. They will also be easy to find.

TOILETRIES

19. STASHING TOILETRIES

Carry only absolute necessities. Airline rules dictate
that for one carry-on bag, liquids and gels must be in
3.4 ounce (100ml) bottles or less, and must be packed
in a one quart zip-lock bag. If you are planning to stay
in a hotel, the basic things will be provided for you.
It's best is to buy the rest from the local market at
your destination.

20. TAKE ALONG TAMPONS

Tampons are a hard to find item in a lot of countries.
Figure out how many you need and pack accordingly.
For longer stays you can buy them online and have
them delivered to where you are staying.

21. GET PAMPERED BEFORE YOU TRAVEL

Some avid travellers suggest getting a pedicure and
manicure just the day before travelling. This not only
gives you a well kept look, you also save the trouble
of packing nail polish. Remember, every little bit of
weight reduced adds up.

ELECTRONICS

22. LUGGING ALONG ELECTRONICS

Electronics have a large role to play in our lives today. Most of us cannot imagine our lives away from our phones, laptops or tablets. However while travelling, one must consider the amount of weight these electronics add to our luggage. Thankfully smart phones come along with all the essentials tools like a camera, email access, picture editing tools and more. They are smart to the point of eliminating the need to carry multiple gadgets. Choose a smart phone that suits all your requirements and travel with the world in your palms or pocket.

23. REDUCE THE NUMBER OF CHARGERS

If you do travel with multiple electronic devices, you will have to bear the additional burden of carrying all their chargers too. Check if a single charger can be used for multiple devices. You might also consider investing in a pocket charger. These small devices support multiple devices while keeping you charged on the go.

24. TRAVEL FRIENDLY APPS

Along with smart phones come numerous apps, which are immensely helpful in our travels. You name it and you have an app for it at hand – take pictures, sharing with friends and family, torch to light dark roads, maps, checking flight/train times, find hotels and many other things. Use these smart alternatives to traditional items like books to eliminate weight and save space.

I get ideas about what's essential
when packing my suitcase.

-Diane von Furstenberg

TRAVELLING WITH KIDS

25. BRING ALONG THE STROLLER

Kids might enjoy walking for a while but they soon tire out and a stroller is the just the right thing for them to rest in while you continue your tour. Strollers also double duty as a luggage carrier and shopping bag holder. Remember to pick a light weight, easy to handle brand of stroller. Better yet, find out in advance if you can rent a stroller at your destination.

26. BRING ONLY ENOUGH DIAPERS FOR YOUR TRIP

Diapers take up a lot of space and add to the weight of your luggage. Therefore it is advisable to carry just enough diapers to last through the trip and a few for afterwards, till you buy fresh stock at your destination. Unless of course you are travelling to a really remote area, in which case you have no choice but to carry the load. Otherwise diapers are something you will find pretty easily.

27. TAKE ONLY A COUPLE OF TOYS

Children are easily attracted by new things in their environment. While travelling they will find numerous 'new' objects to scrutinize and play with. Packing just one favorite toy is enough, or if there is no favorite toy leave out all of them in favor of stories or imaginary games.

28. CARRY KID FRIENDLY SNACKS

Create a small snack counter in your bag to store away quick bites for those sudden hunger pangs. Depending on the child's age this could include chocolates, raisins, dry fruits, granola bars or biscuits. Also keep a bottle of water handy for your little one.

These things do not add much weight and can be adjusted in a handbag or knapsack.

29. GAMES TO CARRY

Create some travel specific, imaginary games if you have slightly grown up children, like spot the attractions. Keep a coloring book and colors handy for in-flight or hotel time. Apps on your smart phone can keep the children engaged with cartoons and story books. Older children are often entertained by games available on phones or tablets. This cuts the weight of luggage down while keeping the kids entertained.

30. LET THE KIDS CARRY THEIR LOAD

A good thing is to start early sharing of responsibilities. Let your child pick a bag of his or her choice and pack it themselves. Keep tabs on what they are stuffing in their bags by asking if they will be using that item on the trip. It could start out being just an entertainment bag initially but with growing years they will learn to sort the useful from the superfluous. Children as little as four can maneuver a small trolley suitcase like a pro- their experience in pull along toys credit. If you are worried that you may be pulling it for them, you may want to start with a backpack.

31. DECIDE ON LOCATION FOR CHILDREN TO SLEEP

While on a trip you might not always get a crib at your destination, and carrying one will make life all the more difficult. Instead call ahead to see if there are any cribs or roll out beds for children. You may even put blankets on the floor. Weave them a story about camping and they will gladly sleep without any trouble.

32. GET BABY PRODUCTS DELIVERED AT YOUR DESTINATION

If you are absolutely paranoid about not getting your favourite variety of diaper or brand of baby food, check out online stores like amazon.com for services in your destination city. You can buy things online ahead of your travel and get them delivered to your hotel upon arrival.

33. FEEDING NEEDS OF YOUR INFANTS

If you are travelling with a breastfed infant, you save the trouble of carrying bottles and bottle sanitization kits. For special food, or medications, you may need to call ahead to make sure you have a refrigerator where you are staying.

34. FEEDING NEEDS OF YOUR TODDLER

With the progression from infancy to toddler, their dietary requirements too evolve. You will have to pack some snacks for travelling time. Fresh fruits and vegetables can be purchased at your destination. Most of the cities you travel to in whichever part of the world, will have baby food products and formulas, available at the local drug-store or the supermarket.

35. PICKING CLOTHES FOR YOUR BABY

Contrary to popular belief, babies can do without many changes of clothes. At the most pack 2 outfits per day. Pack mix and match type clothes for your little one as well. Pick things which are comfortable to wear and quick to dry.

36. SELECTING SHOES FOR YOUR BABY

Like outfits, kids can make do with two pairs of comfortable shoes. If you can get some water resistant shoes it will be best. To expedite drying wet shoes, you can stuff newspaper in them then wrap them with newspaper and leave them to dry overnight.

37. KEEP ONE CHANGE OF CLOTHES HANDY

Travelling with kids can be tricky. Keep a change of clothes for the kids and mum handy in your purse or tote bag. This takes a bit of space in your hand luggage but comes extremely handy in case there are any accidents or spills.

38. LEAVE BEHIND BABY ACCESSORIES

Baby accessories like their bed, bath tub, car seat, crib etc. should be left at home. Many hotels provide a crib on request, while car seats can be borrowed from friends or rented. Babies can be given a bath in the hotel sink or even in the adult bath tub with a little bit of water. If you bring a few bath toys, they can be used in the bath, pool, and out of water. They can also be sanitized easily in the sink.

39. CARRY A SMALL LOAD OF PLASTIC BAGS

With children around there are chances of a number of soiled clothes and diapers. These plastic bags help to sort the dirt from the clean inside your big bag.

These are very light weight and come in handy to other carry stuff as well at times.

PACK WITH A PURPOSE

40. PACKING FOR BUSINESS TRIPS

One neutral-colored suit should suffice. It can be paired with different shirts, ties and accessories for different occasions. One pair of black suit pants could be worn with a matching jacket for the office or with a snazzy top for dinner.

41. PACKING FOR A CRUISE

Most cruises have formal dinners, and that formal dress usually takes up a lot of space. However you might find a tuxedo to rent. For women, a short black dress with multiple accessory options will do the trick.

42. PACKING FOR A LONG TRIP OVER DIFFERENT CLIMATES

The secret packing mantra for travel over multiple climates is layering. Layering traps air around your body creating insulation against the cold. The same light t-shirt that is comfortable in a warmer climate can be the innermost layer in a colder climate.

REDUCE SOME MORE WEIGHT

43. LEAVE PRECIOUS THINGS AT HOME

Things that you would hate to lose or get damaged leave them at home. Precious jewelry, expensive gadgets or dresses, could be anything. You will not require these on your trip. Leave them at home and spare the load on your mind.

44. SEND SOUVENIRS BY MAIL

If you have spent all your money on purchasing souvenirs, carrying them back in the same bag that you brought along would be difficult. Either pack everything in another bag and check it in the airport or get everything shipped to your home. Use an international carrier for a secure transit, but this could be more expensive than the checking fees at the airport.

45. AVOID CARRYING BOOKS

Books equal to weight. There are many reading apps which you can download on your smart phone or tab.

Plus there are gadgets like Kindle and Nook that are thinner and lighter alternatives to your regular book.

CHECK, GET, SET, CHECK AGAIN

46. STRATEGIZE BEFORE PACKING

Create a travel list and prepare all that you think you need to carry along. Keep everything on your bed or floor before packing and then think through once again – do I really need that? Any item that meets this question can be avoided. Remove whatever you don't really need and pack the rest.

47. TEST YOUR LUGGAGE

Once you have fully packed for the trip take a test trip with your luggage. Take your bags and go to town for window shopping for an hour. If you enjoy your hour long trip it is good to go, if not, go home and reduce the load some more. Repeat this test till you hit the right weight.

48. ADD A ROLL OF DUCT TAPE

You might wonder why, when this book has been talking about reducing stuff, we're suddenly asking you to pack something totally unusual. This is because when you have limited supplies, duct tape is immensely helpful for small repairs – a broken bag, leaking zip-lock bag, broken sunglasses, you name it and duct tape can fix it, temporarily.

49. LIST OF ESSENTIAL ITEMS

Even though the emphasis is on packing light, there are things which have to be carried for any trip. Here is our list of essentials:

• Passport/Visa or any other ID

• Any other paper work that might be required on a trip like permits, hotel reservation confirmations etc.

• Medicines – all your prescription medicines and emergency kit, especially if you are travelling with children

• Medical or vaccination records

• Money in foreign currency if travelling to a different country

• Tickets- Email or Message them to your phone

50. MAKE THE MOST OF YOUR TRIP

Wherever you are going, whatever you hope to do we encourage you to embrace it whole-heartedly. Take in the scenery, the culture and above all, enjoy your time away from home.

On a long journey even a straw weighs heavy.

-Spanish Proverb

PACKING AND PLANNING TIPS

A Week before Leaving

- Arrange for someone to take care of pets and water plants.

- Stop mail and newspaper.

- Notify Credit Card companies where you are going.

- Change your thermostat settings.

- Car inspected, oil is changed, and tires have the correct pressure.

- Passports and photo identification is up to date.

- Pay bills.

- Copy important items and download travel Apps.

- Start collecting small bills for tips.

Right Before Leaving

- Clean out refrigerator.

- Empty garbage cans.

- Lock windows.

- Make sure you have the proper identification with you.

- Bring cash for tips.

- Remember travel documents.

- Lock door behind you.

- Remember wallet.

- Unplug items in house and pack chargers.

READ OTHER
GREATER THAN A TOURIST
BOOKS

Greater Than a Tourist San Miguel de Allende Guanajuato Mexico:
50 Travel Tips from a Local by Tom Peterson

Greater Than a Tourist – Lake George Area New York USA:
50 Travel Tips from a Local by Janine Hirschklau

Greater Than a Tourist – Monterey California United States:
50 Travel Tips from a Local by Katie Begley

Greater Than a Tourist – Chanai Crete Greece:
50 Travel Tips from a Local by Dimitra Papagrigoraki

Greater Than a Tourist – The Garden Route Western Cape Province
South Africa: 50 Travel Tips from a Local by Li-Anne McGregor van
Aardt

Greater Than a Tourist – Sevilla Andalusia Spain:
50 Travel Tips from a Local by Gabi Gazon

Greater Than a Tourist – Kota Bharu Kelantan Malaysia:
50 Travel Tips from a Local by Aditi Shukla

Children's Book: Charlie the Cavalier Travels the World by Lisa
Rusczyk

> TOURIST

Visit Greater Than a Tourist for Free Travel Tips
http://GreaterThanATourist.com

Sign up for the Greater Than a Tourist Newsletter for
discount days, new books, and travel information:
http://eepurl.com/cxspyf

Follow us on Facebook for tips, images, and ideas:
https://www.facebook.com/GreaterThanATourist

Follow us on Pinterest for travel tips and ideas:
http://pinterest.com/GreaterThanATourist

Follow us on Instagram for beautiful travel images:
http://Instagram.com/GreaterThanATourist

>TOURIST

> TOURIST

Please leave your honest review of this book on Amazon and Goodreads. Please send your feedback to GreaterThanaTourist@gmail.com as we continue to improve the series. We appreciate your positive and constructive feedback. Thank you.

METRIC CONVERSIONS

TEMPERATURE

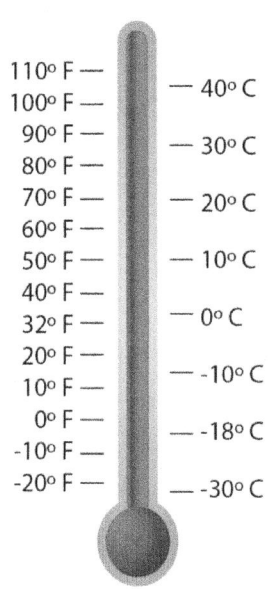

110° F —
100° F —   — 40° C
90° F —
80° F —   — 30° C
70° F —   — 20° C
60° F —
50° F —   — 10° C
40° F —
32° F —   — 0° C
20° F —
10° F —   — -10° C
0° F —   — -18° C
-10° F —
-20° F —   — -30° C

To convert F to C:

Subtract 32, and then multiply by 5/9 or .5555.

To Convert C to F:

Multiply by 1.8 and then add 32.

32F = 0C

LIQUID VOLUME

To Convert:...............Multiply by

U.S. Gallons to Liters............... 3.8
U.S. Liters to Gallons 26
Imperial Gallons to U.S. Gallons 1.2
Imperial Gallons to Liters....... 4.55
Liters to Imperial Gallons 22
1 Liter = .26 U.S. Gallon
1 U.S. Gallon = 3.8 Liters

DISTANCE

To convert ....Multiply by

Inches to Centimeters 2.54
Centimeters to Inches 39
Feet to Meters...................... .3
Meters to Feet 3.28
Yards to Meters 91
Meters to Yards 1.09
Miles to Kilometers 1.61
Kilometers to Miles............ .62
1 Mile = 1.6 km
1 km = .62 Miles

WEIGHT

1 Ounce = .28 Grams
1 Pound = .4555 Kilograms
1 Gram = .04 Ounce
1 Kilogram = 2.2 Pounds

TRAVEL QUESTIONS

- Do you bring presents home to family or friends after a vacation?

- Do you get motion sick?

- Do you have a favorite billboard?

- Do you know what to do if there is a flat tire?

- Do you like a sun roof open?

- Do you like to eat in the car?

- Do you like to wear sun glasses in the car?

- Do you like toppings on your ice cream?

- Do you use public bathrooms?

- Did you bring your cell phone and does it have power?

- Do you have a form of identification with you?

- Have you ever been pulled over by a cop?

- Have you ever given money to a stranger on a road trip?

- Have you ever taken a road trip with animals?

- Have you ever went on a vacation alone?

- Have you ever run out of gas?

- If you could move to any place in the world, where would it be?

- If you could travel anywhere in the world, where would you travel?

- If you could travel in any vehicle, which one would it be?

- If you had three things to wish for from a magic genie, what would they be?

- If you have a driver's license, how many times did it take you to pass the test?

- What are you the most afraid of on vacation?

- What do you want to get away from the most when you are on vacation?

- What foods smells bad to you?

- What item do you bring on ever trip with you away from home?

- What makes you sleepy?

- What song would you love to hear on the radio when you're cruising on the highway?

- What travel job would you want the least?

- What will you miss most while you are away from home?

- What is something you always wanted to try?

- What is the best road side attraction that you ever saw?

- What is the farthest distance you ever biked?

- What is the farthest distance you ever walked?

- What is the weirdest thing you needed to buy while on vacation?

- What is your favorite candy?

- What is your favorite color car?

- What is your favorite family vacation?

- What is your favorite food?

- What is your favorite gas station drink or food?

- What is your favorite license plate design?

- What is your favorite restaurant?

- What is your favorite smell?

- What is your favorite song?

- What is your favorite sound that nature makes?

- What is your favorite thing to bring home from a vacation?

- What is your favorite vacation with friends?

- What is your favorite way to relax?

- Where is the farthest place you ever traveled in a car?

- Where is the farthest place you ever went North, South, East and West?

- Where is your favorite place in the world?

- Who is your favorite singer?

- Who taught you how to drive?

- Who will you miss the most while you are away?

- Who if the first person you will contact when you get to your destination?

- Who brought you on your first vacation?

- Who likes to travel the most in your life?

- Would you rather be hot or cold?

- Would you rather drive above, below, or at the speed limited?

- Would you rather drive on a highway or a back road?

- Would you rather go on a train or a boat?

- Would you rather go to the beach or the woods?

TRAVEL BUCKET LIST

1.

2.

3.

4.

5.

6.

7.

8.

9.

10.

NOTES

Printed in Great Britain
by Amazon

80608081R00072